MEMORIZING
Holy Scripture

Meditate on Bible Verses While Coloring Fun Illustrations

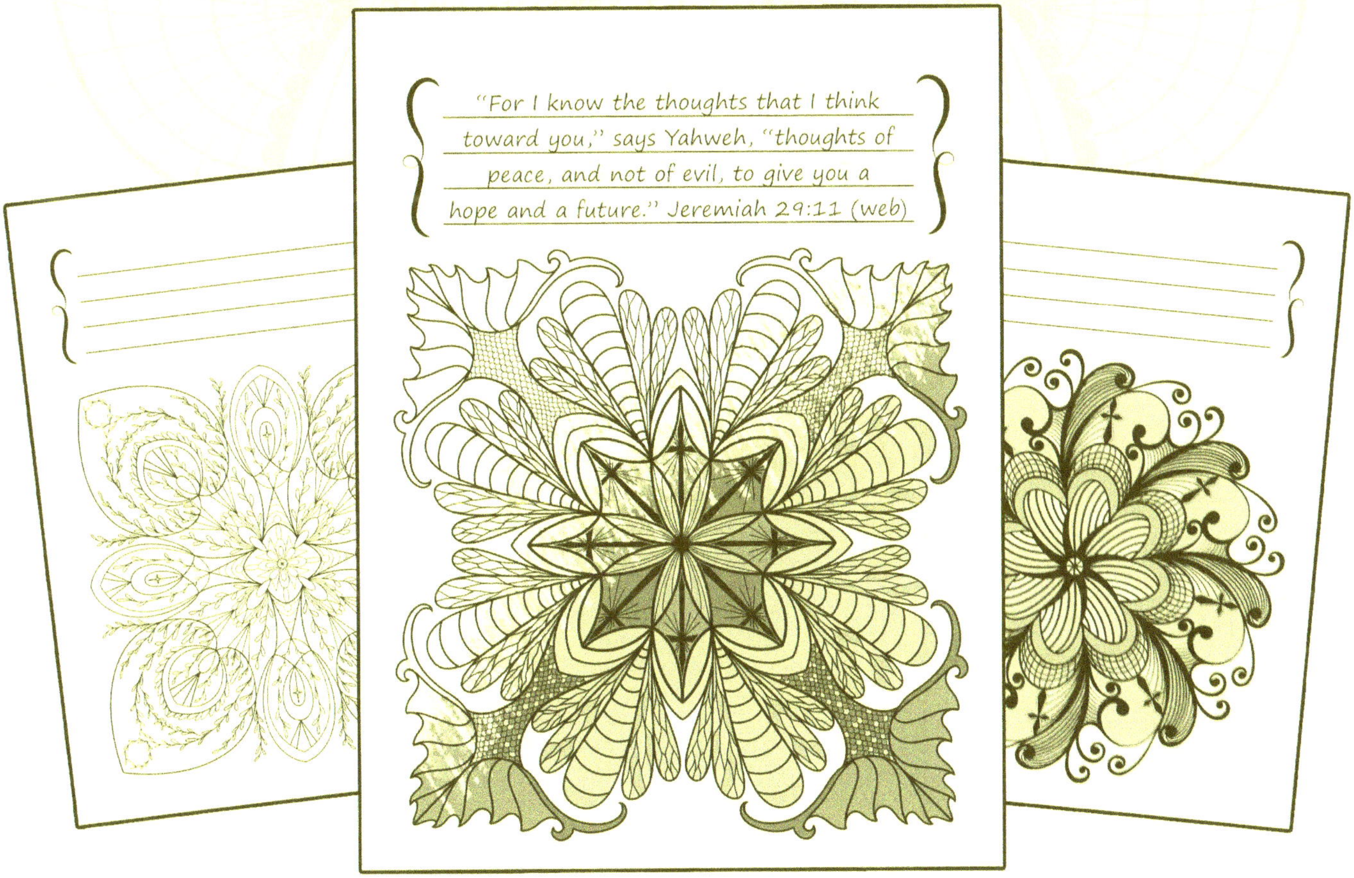

"For I know the thoughts that I think toward you," says Yahweh, "thoughts of peace, and not of evil, to give you a hope and a future." Jeremiah 29:11 (web)

A NAOMI RAYE PUBLICATION

Knowing the Word of God is very important in living the Christian life. It helps us remember who God is, both in good times and bad, and the promises He has made to us throughout the Holy Bible.

This coloring book provides you an opportunity to meditate on different Bible verses as you live out your relationship with the Lord. Each page has lines for you to write down your chosen Bible verse. Each page will also have a beautiful detailed illustration that you will color while meditating on the Scripture you wrote down. This repetition will help you to memorize the Scripture so you can have the Word of God written on your heart!

I hope you enjoy filling this book with lots of color and the Word of God while filling your heart with a deeper understanding and love for our Lord Jesus Christ.

Some Bible Verses Every Christian Should Know:

Psalms 91:11-12	Matthew 18:20	1 Corinthians 10:31
John 3:16-17	Mark 12:30-31	The Lord's Prayer
Luke 9:23	Luke 6:37-38	Luke 11:2-4
John 8:31-32	John 14:6	1 Corinthians 10:23
John 11:25	Romans 5:8	2 Corinthians 5:7
John 14:6	Romans 6:23	2 Corinthians 12:7-10
John 15:13-14	Romans 8:1	Galatians 5:22-23
Matthew 6:14-15	Romans 8:28	Ephesians 2:8-9
Matthew 6:21	Romans 10:12-13	Ephesians 4:32
Matthew 6:31-33	Romans 12:2	Jeremiah 29:11-12
Matthew 11:28-30	1 Corinthians 10:13	Philippians 4:13

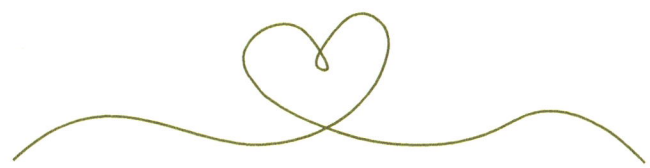

This list is not by any means exhaustive, as the Bible is God's Holy word and is all worth memorizing. So, whether you are a new Christian or have been one for many years, I hope this coloring book makes memorizing your favorite Bible verses not only easier, but a little more fun as well.

{ _____
  _____
  _____
  _____ }

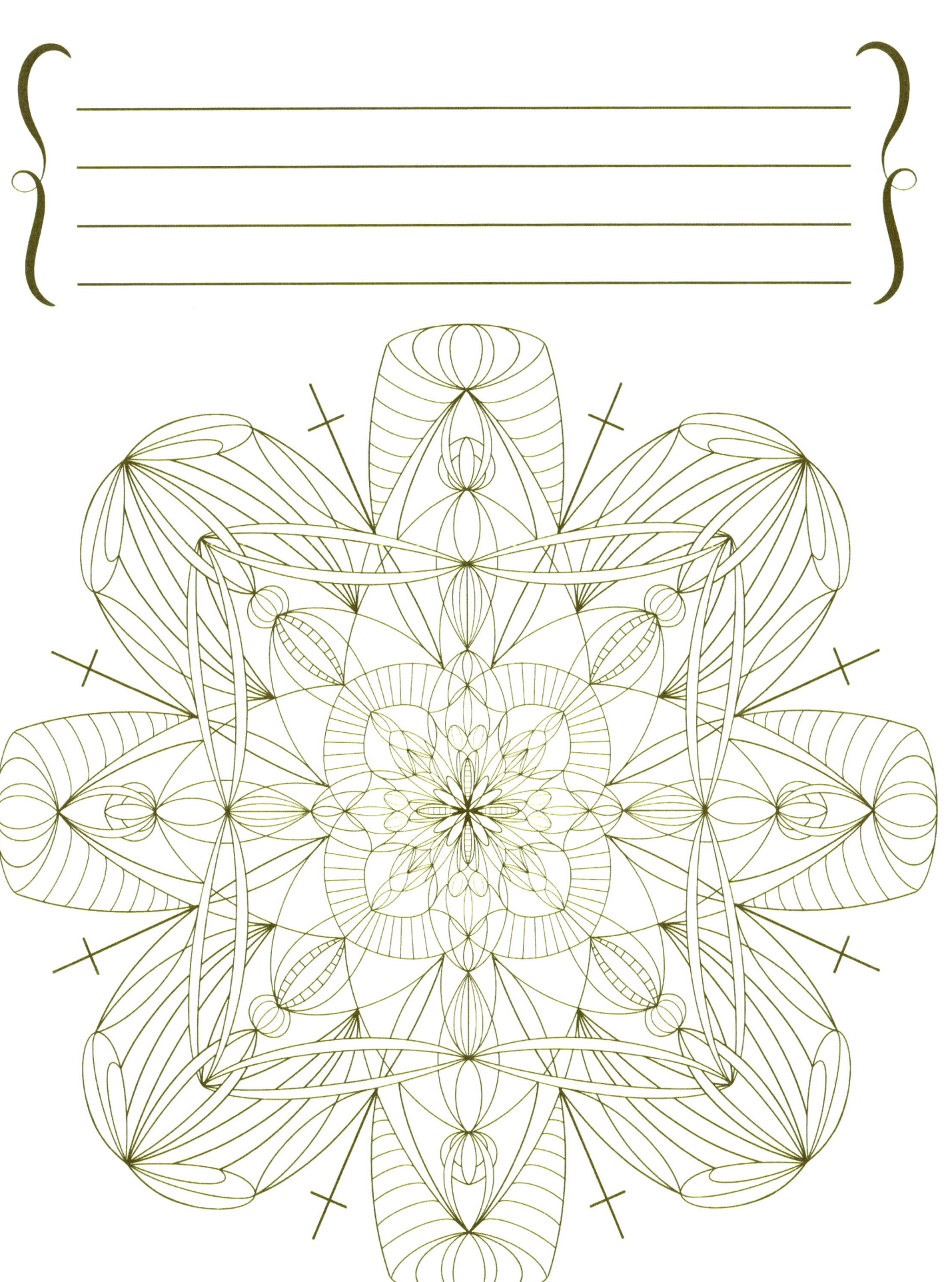

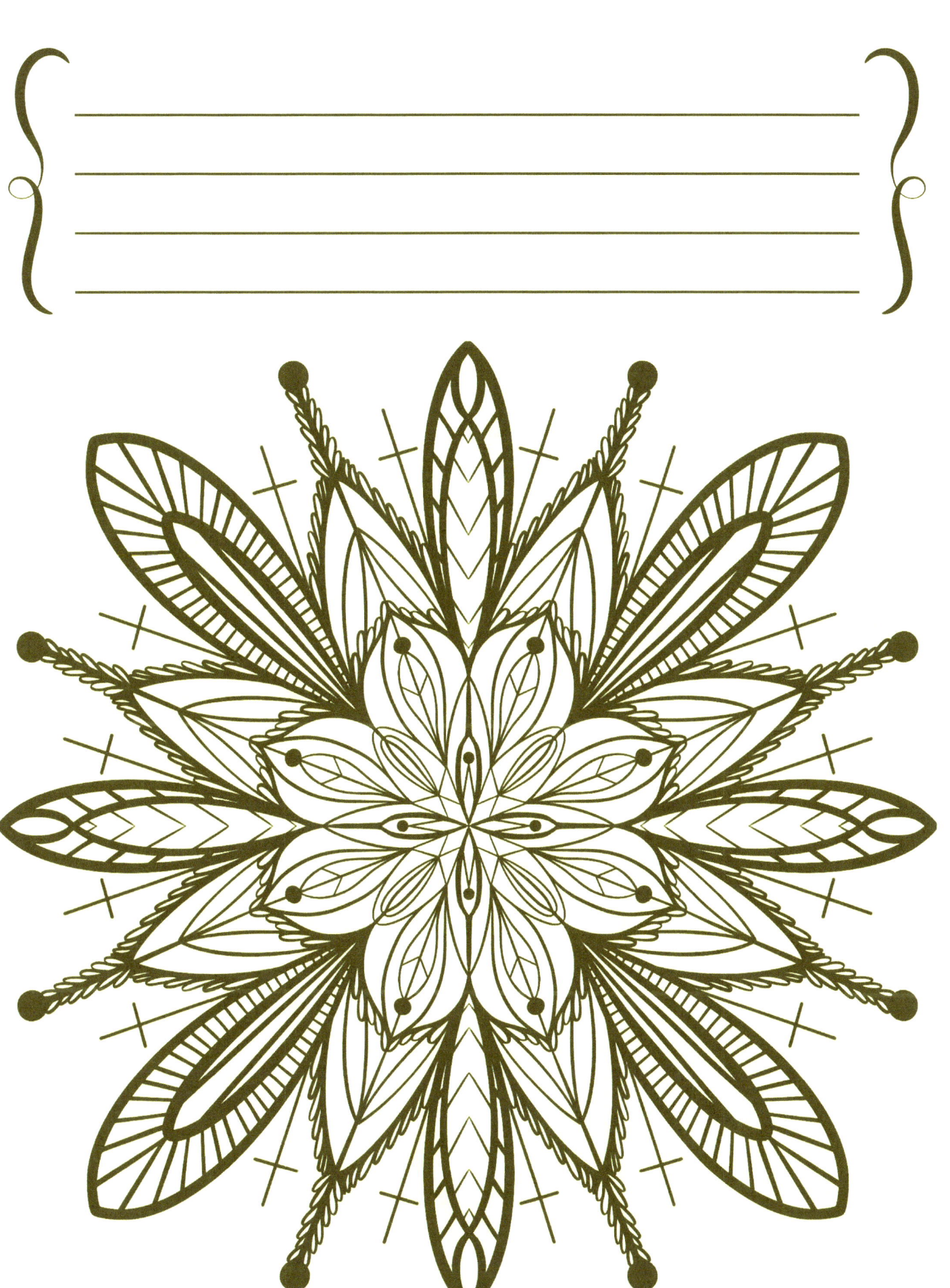

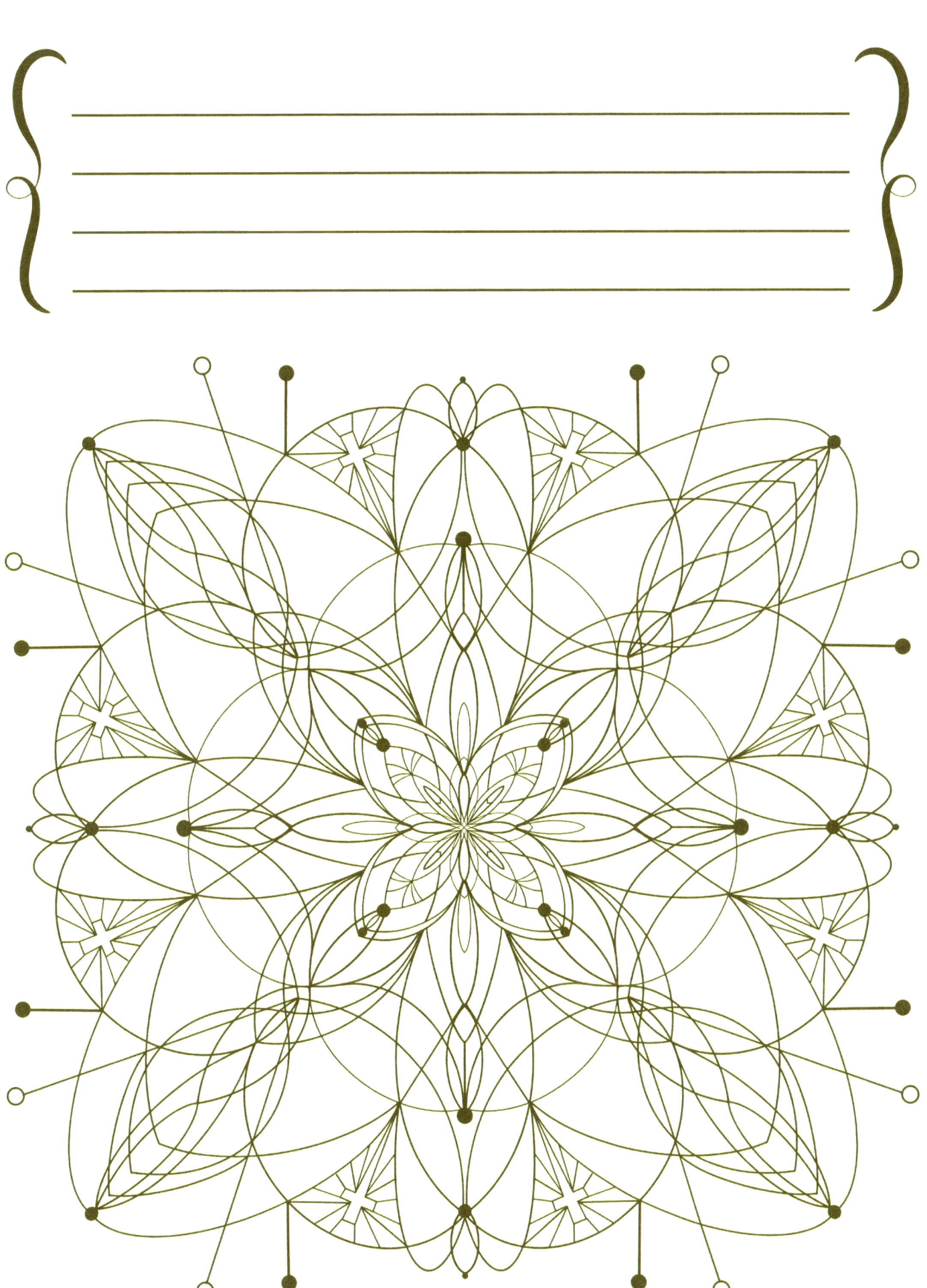

{ _____
  _____
  _____
  _____ }

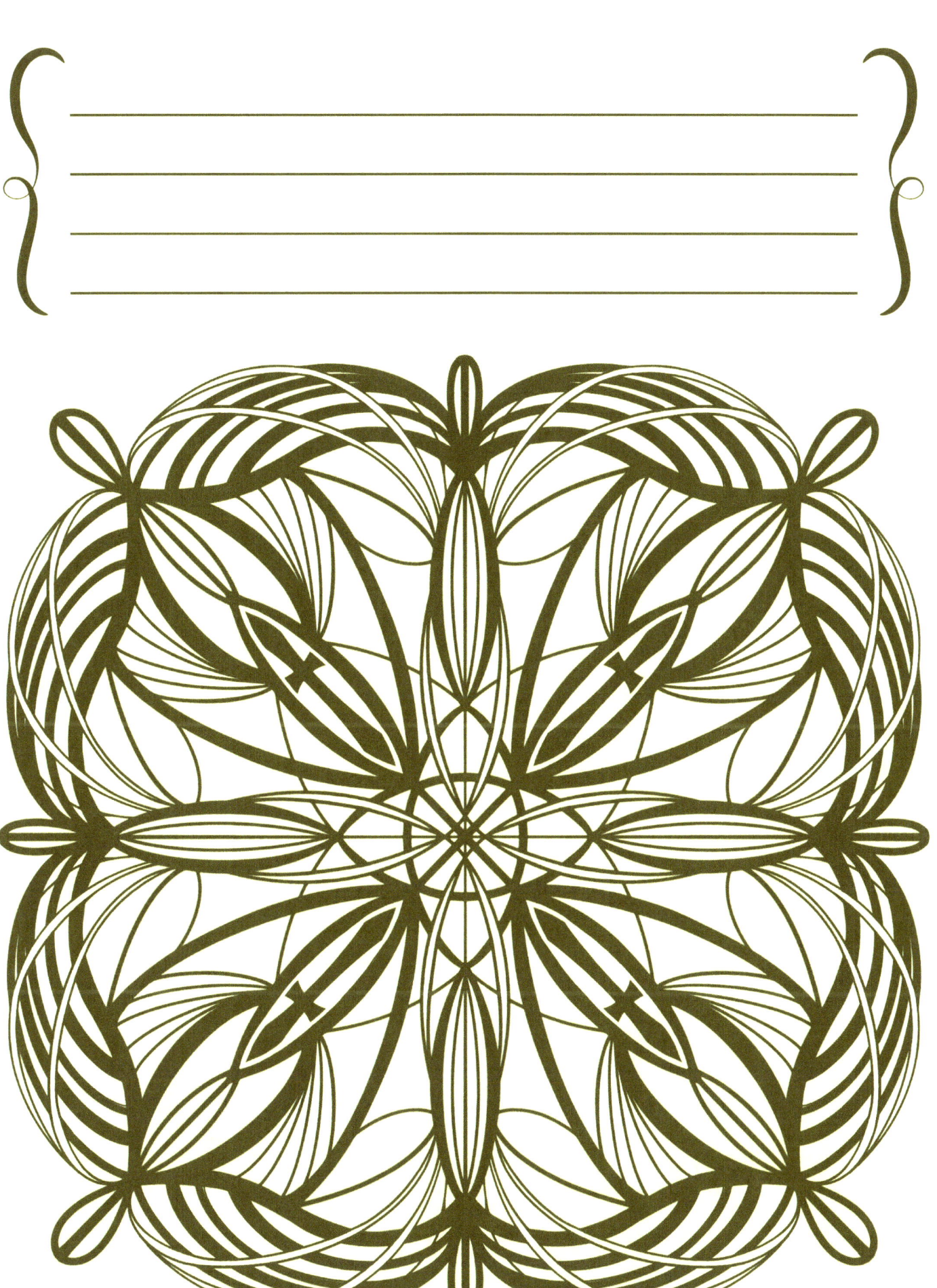

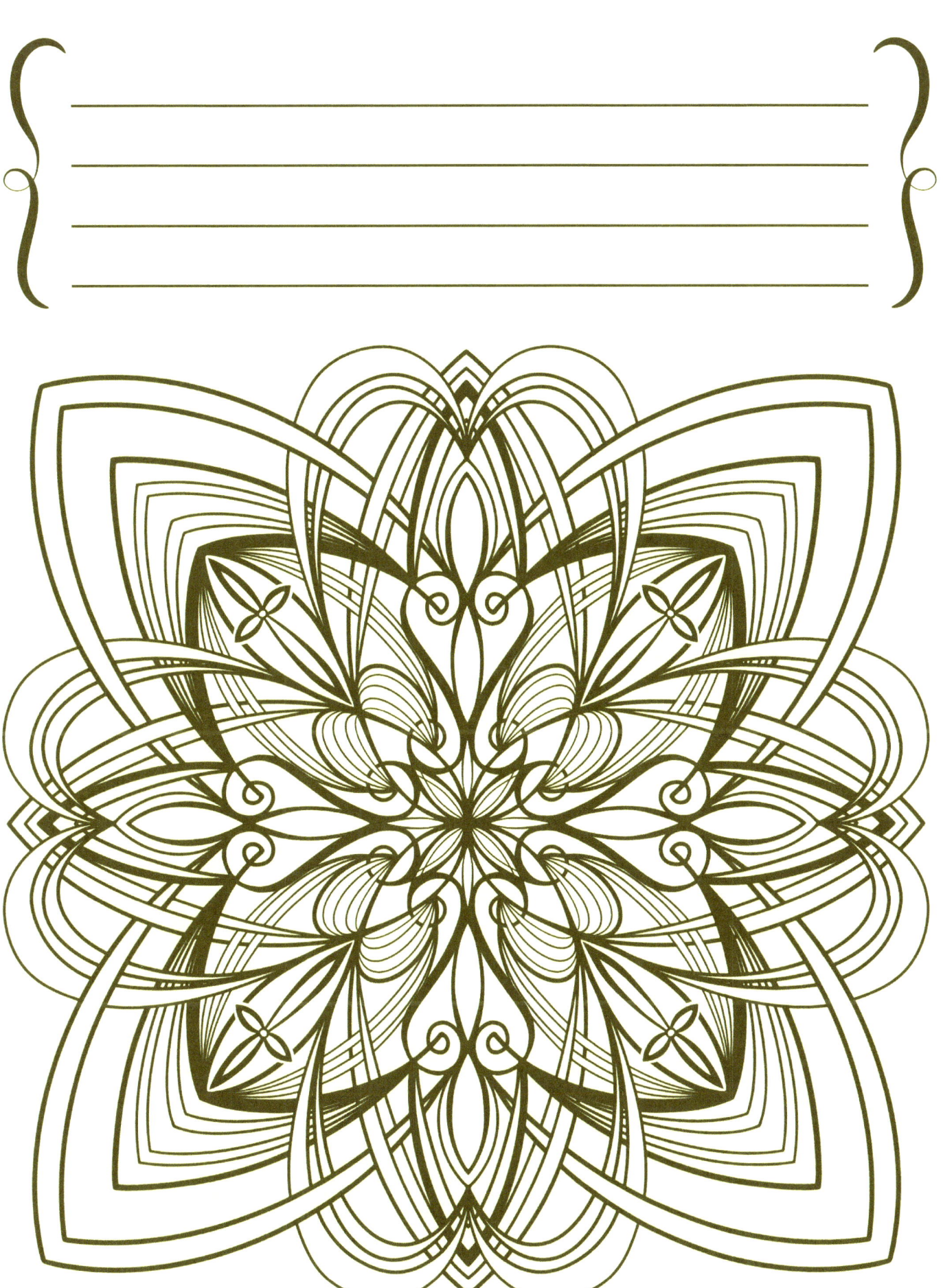

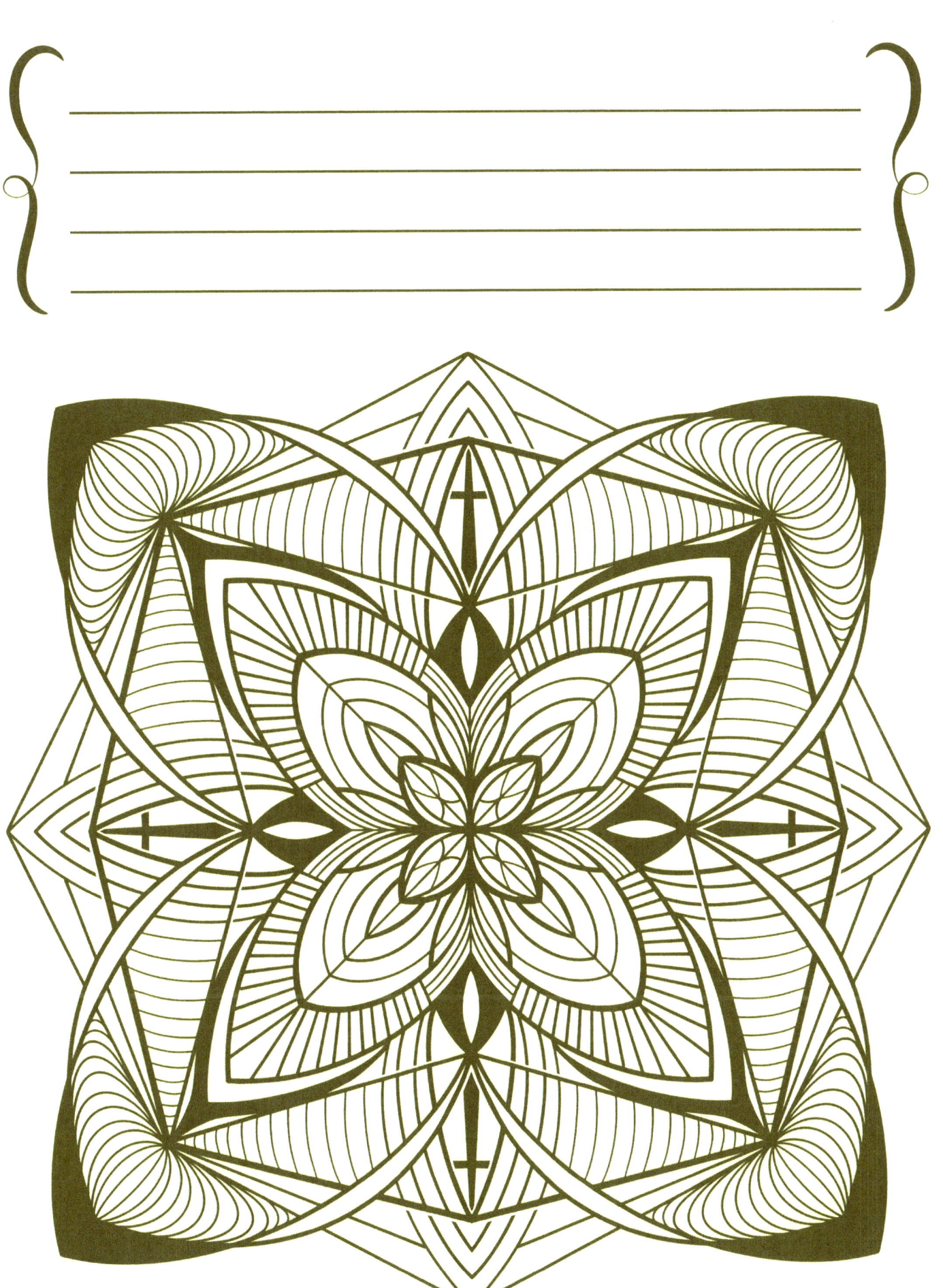

{ _____ }

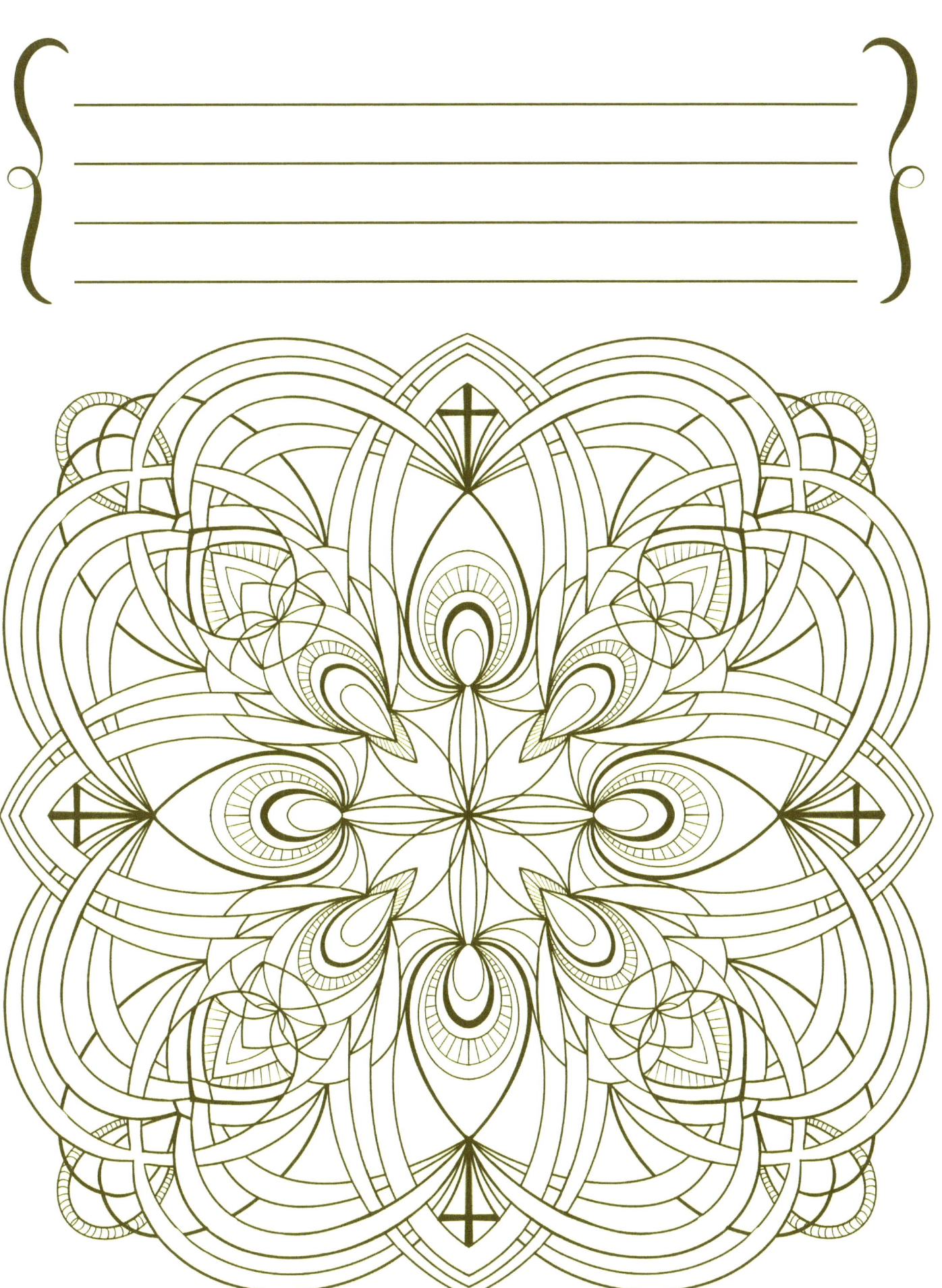

www.ingramcontent.com/pod-product-compliance
Lightning Source LLC
Chambersburg PA
CBHW080436220526
45465CB00019B/2477